Making BREADS
with Home-grown
YEASTS
& Home-ground
GRAINS

by PHYLLIS HOBSO

A Garden Way Guide
of HOMESTEAD RECIPES

GARDEN WAY PUBLISHING
CHARLOTTE, VERMONT 05445

Library of Congress Catalog Card Number: 74-75468
ISBN: 0-88266-032-2
COPYRIGHT 1974 BY GARDEN WAY PUBLISHING CO.
Second Printing, April 1975

Format and drawings by Frank Lieberman

PRINTED IN THE UNITED STATES

HOME-GROUND GRAINS
& HOME-GROWN YEASTS

Suppose we discovered an almost perfect food. This food is delicious, wholesome and satisfying. It is rich in the B vitamins, vitamin E and iron, the nutrients most lacking in our daily diets.

In addition, this food can be combined with milk and eggs and honey to make an endless variety of delicious, nutritious foods which keep well, combine with other foods and can be cooked in advance to be convenient for every meal.

Most unbelievable of all, this food costs so little and keeps so well without refrigeration that we could buy a year's supply at a time and keep it on hand, ready to be ground and cooked as we need it.

We're intelligent people. We would accept such a food gratefully and would happily enjoy its benefits every day. Right? Wrong. Incredibly, many of us refuse this almost perfect food and choose instead a tasteless, weightless, non-nutritional substitute which is far more expensive.

The almost perfect food, of course, is whole grains, which must be ground just before they are cooked to be at their most flavorful, nutritious best. Until they are ground, they will keep indefinitely, if they are cool and dry. After grinding, every hour's exposure to air means a loss of vitamins and flavor.

But they are worth the trouble. Home-ground grains, used with home-grown yeast, are truly the staff of life. Man could live in good health on nothing more than well-made bread and fresh fruits and vegetables. And yet few of us eat home-ground grains. Even those of us who raise most or all of our food shy away from raising grains.

Every homestead has a garden where fresh vegetables are raised. Most have a berry patch and a few trees to grow fresh fruits. Some have a barnyard and a few chickens for eggs and meat, a calf and a pig or two, plus a cow or some goats for milk. But few homesteaders raise their own grain, although almost any family with a little land could raise enough wheat and corn and oats for its own use.

GROWING YOUR OWN WHEAT

One-fourth of an acre of rich, fertile land should produce at least five bushels of wheat, more than a year's supply for the average family. Wheat requires well-fertilized soil, so prepare the plot in advance by plowing under barn manure, then sowing a cover crop of rye. In the spring, work under this cover crop and till the soil to a fine bed.

Planting — On this prepared bed, broadcast (by hand or with a broadcast seeder) one peck of seed to the one-fourth acre. Walk with a medium pace as you seed. You can leave the seed uncovered, but it will germinate better if you can roll it down.

The time to plant wheat depends on the variety, which depends on the climate and the soil. Here in the midwest, we plant hard winter wheat in September and harvest it the following July. But some wheats are planted in the spring and harvested in the fall. You local County Agent will know the variety and time for planting in your area. He can also tell you where to obtain seed.

Once the seed is planted, it's up to the sun and the rain. Wheat will sprout within a week and soon will look like bright green grass. In every stage, wheat is one of the most attractive crops, so it would not be unpleasant near the house. As it matures, the green stalks grow two or two-and-one-half feet tall, then turn golden. When it has passed the peak of its golden color and turns tan, the wheat is ready for harvest. You can test it by tasting a grain. It should be hard, yet soft enough to be dented with pressure from a fingernail. And it should have a nut-like flavor.

Harvesting — If you let your wheat reach this past-its-golden-prime color, you can skip the step of shocking it in the field to dry, although this is the most picturesque stage. If you want to shock your wheat, cut the stalks, tie them into bundles and stand them in the sun to dry for a week to 10 days.

Either way, you're now ready for threshing. You can vent your frustrations on it, as the European peasants used to do, by laying the stalks out on a hard surface and flailing them, or you can do it in half the time with half the effort by beating the kernels directly into a barrel.

As you cut each bundle, hold it, head down, in the barrel and hit it several times sharply against the sides to knock off the kernels of wheat. When most of the kernels have fallen into the barrel, break or cut off the end of the stalks and toss them to the chickens, which will finish threshing them for you. Save the stalks. They're called straw, and it makes fine barn bedding for the winter ahead.

If the wheat in the barrel is "dirty" (mixed with chaff), you'll need to winnow it. You can make a big production of this with a sheet of canvas and a fanning mill; you can toss the grains of wheat into the air on a windy day, or you can do as we do — simply pick the weed seeds out of each cupful just before we grind it into flour, which is just before we make bread.

Storing — Whatever you do, though, don't let anyone talk you into washing the wheat. Unless you sprayed your wheat with pesticides, it isn't necessary. And if you did, washing it won't take care of the poisons. Under home drying conditions, washed wheat is almost certain to become moldy wheat.

RAISING OTHER GRAINS

Other small grains — oats, rye and barley — are grown and harvested much the same as wheat. Soybeans are planted, cared for and harvested just as you would any dried beans.

Corn — Although the average family uses less corn meal than wheat flour, growing and drying some corn for grinding is well worth the small amount of trouble. Any corn variety will do. We just leave some of the sweet corn in the garden to dry, but you could plant a small patch by the wheat field. Either way, you simply leave it there to dry naturally. It should be dry enough to grind by first frost, but if you don't get around to it then, it can stand until spring. If the weather — or your climate — is wet enough to cause mold, you can hang the ears, encased in their husks, in a shed to dry.

Corn keeps indefinitely on the cob, or it can be shelled and stored in gallon glass jars in a cool place. Like the small grains, corn should be ground just before using.

OTHER SOURCES

But even if you don't have the land you can enjoy the luxury of homeground grains. Wheat and rye berries, soybeans and rolled oats are sold at most health food stores, or can be ordered by mail from any of the following:

Walnut Acres
R.D. 1
Penns Creek, Pa. 17862

Arrowhead Mills
P.O. Box 866
Hereford, Texas 79045

Natural Development Co.
Box 215
Bainbridge, Pa. 17502

Better Foods Foundation Inc.
200 N. Washington St.
Greencastle, Pa. 17225

Vermont Country Store
Weston, Vt. 05161

But you can buy them much cheaper at the source. If you live in a part of the country where these grains are grown, you can arrange with a local farmer to buy a few bushels at harvest time, before it goes into storage where it is fumigated. It would be worth the time and cost to make arrangements by mail and travel even a hundred miles, if necessary, to pick up a year's supply of grains.

STORING

How much? We use four bushels of wheat, one bushel of oats and two bushels of shelled corn a year. Soy beans, which are not grains, but are used with grains, can also be bought by the bushel here in the midwest. All of them store safely in clean, sunned-and-aired, metal garbage cans with tight-fitting lids. They keep well in our food storage room all year. Any grains left over the following summer are taken to the barn and mixed with the livestock feed.

GRINDING

Grinding is no problem. Home flour mills — even the fancy ones with stone grinding wheels — cost about the same as any good kitchen appliance. The price of hand-cranked models ranges from about $15 to $50. Electric models run from $100 to $200. The crank models require a little muscle, but the electric ones are as easy to use as a blender. As a matter of fact, a blender can be used in a pinch.

The crank models with metal blades will grind any grain (or soybeans) to a fine meal. This (and the blender-ground grain) is not really a flour, but can be combined half and half with commercial unbleached flour for a satisfactory substitute.

Stone wheel mills — both electric and hand crank — will produce a fine flour of all grains, but cannot be used to grind soy beans because the oil from the beans will damage the stone.

Equipment Sources — Hand crank grinders can be found in some hardware stores and may be ordered by mail. The following companies manufacture several electric models:

Lee Manufacturing Co.
2021 W. Wisconsin Ave.
Milwaukee, Wisconsin 53201

Smithfield Implement Co.
97 North Main Street
Smithfield, Utah 84335

Retsel Corp.
P.O. Box 291
McCammon, Idaho 83250

HOME GROWN YEAST

Yeast is a plant, a very delicate, fast-growing plant that requires some form of sugar to feed on and a temperature from 70 to 80 degrees in which to grow. Given the proper food and environment, a yeast plant will increase more than 10 times its own volume overnight. But without almost perfect conditions, the yeast plant will die or the medium in which it is growing will sour.

These recipes do not tell you how to "make" yeast, but how to "grow" it.

STARTER OR SPONGE

The main ingredient of yeast is yeast. If you're going to grow yeast, you'll need seed. Any kind of yeast will do. You can start with the store bought kind, cake or dry. After you get your starter going, (also called sponge or ferment), make sure you reserve at least 1 cup each time for the next batch.

Homegrown yeast may be used as a starter from one baking to the next. This mixture is sometimes called a sponge or ferment. Many women in Grandmother's era kept their sponge from one baking to the next for years at a time. Some women proudly spoke of a "sponge" or "starter" they had kept growing for 40 or 50 years. Some were passed down in families from one generation to another.

One cup sponge or starter, 1 cake of yeast or 1 package of dry yeast will make two loaves of bread.

EVERLASTING YEAST

POTATO YEAST

Potato yeast makes a moist, heavy bread because the potato helps absorb the moisture and adds nutrition.

Peel, boil and mash 4 potatoes. Add 4 tablespoons sugar, 1 tablespoon ginger, 1 tablespoon salt, 2 cups flour and 2 cups boiling water. Beat until all lumps disappear. When it has cooled to lukewarm, add 1 cup yeast and set aside to rise. Stir down and store in a stone jar in a cool place.

OR

Peel and chop 3 medium potatoes. Cook until tender. Mash and blend with potato water and enough cold water to make 3 cups. Add ¼ cup honey and cool to lukewarm. Add 1 cup starter reserved from the last baking or 1 package dried yeast soaked in 1 cup lukewarm water. Let stand in a warm place overnight. In the morning, refrigerate 1 cup starter for the next baking and use remainder for any recipe for 4 loaves.

OR

Peel and cube 3 large or 4 medium potatoes. Cook until tender in 2 cups water. Mash, using the cooking water. Add ½ cup honey, 2 teaspoons salt and 2 cups water cool enough to make the mixture lukewarm. Then add 1 cup yeast starter and mix well. Allow to stand overnight, covered. In the morning, stir down and use 1 cup for baking. Store the remainder in a crock in a cool place.

OR

Pare and grate 4 large potatoes in 1 quart boiling water. Boil 5 minutes, stirring constantly. When cool, add ½ cup sugar, 2 tablespoons salt and 1 cake yeast dissolved in ½ cup cool water, or ½ cup yeast starter. Pour mixture into a stone jar, cover and put in a warm place for at least 3 hours, stirring down the mixture each time it comes to the top of the jar. When fermentation has ceased, cover jar closely and store in a cool place.

HOPS YEAST

Hops yeast makes a lighter, fluffier bread with less body than potato yeast. Hops may sometimes be purchased in

HOPS

gourmet and delicatessan shops that specialize in beer-making and wine-making supplies.

Peel, cube and cook 4 medium potatoes. Mash. In the same water, cook 1 cup hops 15 to 20 minutes. Strain out the hops and pour this water, boiling hot, over 2 cups flour. Add ½ cup sugar and 1 teaspoon salt and the mashed potato. Let set in a warm place overnight. In the morning, add 1 cup starter and let ferment.

OR

Cook 12 potatoes in 1 gallon water. Remove and mash the potatoes while 3 cups hops simmer in the potato water. After 15 minutes, strain out the hops and pour the water over the mashed potato. Add 1 cup brown sugar, 1 teaspoon salt and, when cooled to lukewarm, 1 cup yeast starter. Pour into a warm crock, letting it stand uncovered for 24 hours. Then stir down and cover before storing in a cool place.

OR

Boil 1 cup hops in a cloth bag in 2 quarts water for 15 minutes. Remove bag with hops. Add 5 large, peeled and grated potatoes, 1 cup sugar, 1 tablespoon salt and 1 tablespoon ginger. Cook, stirring, 5 to 10 minutes, until mixture thickens. Turn into a jar and cool until lukewarm. Add 1 cup yeast (always save one cup to start the next batch). Until fermentation stops, stir down each time it rises. Cover tightly and set in a cool place. It will keep two weeks.

OR

Take as many hops as can be grasped in the hand twice, put ½ gallon water over them and boil slowly for one hour. Pare and grate 6 large potatoes into a 2-gallon stone crock, add ½ cup sugar, 1 tablespoon each salt and ginger. Pour over this ½ gallon of the boiling hops water, stirring constantly. When the mixture is lukewarm, add 1 cup yeast and set in a warm place to rise. Store in a cool place.

OR

Boil a double handful of hops in 1 gallon water. Boil 15 to 20 minutes, then strain hops from water. Stir flour or corn meal into water until it becomes a thick batter. Let stand until lukewarm, then add 1 cup yeast starter and stir well. Set in a warm place until light. Will keep 10 to 12 days if closed tightly and kept in a cool place.

MALT YEAST

Boil ½ pound hops in 1 gallon water for 30 minutes. Strain out hops, reserving liquid. To this add ½ pound malt flour and boil 10 minutes longer, stirring constantly. Cool to lukewarm and stir in ½ pound brown sugar and 1 cup starter. Pour into a warm crock, cover loosely and set in a warm place to rise overnight. In the morning, stir down and store in a cool place.

FARMER'S YEAST

Take a handful of unpressed hops (those showing the pollen dust are best) and put them into 1 quart of water. Add 4 potatoes and boil until the potatoes are well cooked. Mash all together and strain through a cloth. Add enough flour to make a thick batter. Add 1 teaspoon salt, 1 tablespoon ginger and ½ cup sugar. Set over heat and bring to a boil again, stirring constantly. Set aside to cool. When lukewarm, add 1 cup yeast starter. Use within 1 week.

OR

Mix 1 quart boiling water, 1 cup hops with pollen and 4 peeled, cubed potatoes. Cover and cook until potatoes are tender. Strain out hops and mash potatoes with water. Add enough flour to make a thick batter, ½ cup honey and 1 teaspoon salt. Gradually heat to boiling point, stirring constantly. Cool to lukewarm and add 2 cups starter. Stir. Allow to stand 2 to 3 days, until light and spongy. Store in loosely-covered crock in a cool place.

BRAN YEAST

Add a handful of wheat bran to 2 quarts boiling water and cook, stirring constantly, 15 to 20 minutes. Discard bran and into the strained water stir ½ cup honey and enough flour to make a thick batter. Cool to lukewarm and add 1 cup yeast starter. Keep in a warm place until light, then stir down. Cover and keep in a cool place.

GRAIN YEAST

Finely grind 1 cup each of corn, barley and rye, all sprouting. Mix with water to cover and boil until thick. Cool and add ½ cup honey and enough flour to make a thick batter. Add 1 cup yeast starter. Let rise in a warm place. Let stand 24 hours and remove globules from the surface. Store in a loosely-covered crock in a cool place.

BUTTERMILK YEAST

1 quart buttermilk
flour
½ cup sugar
1 cup yeast
3 pints water

At noon, heat buttermilk to the boiling point. Cool. Add yeast, stir and add enough flour to make a stiff batter. Let stand in a warm place until evening, then add 1½ pints water and let stand until morning. In the morning, add remaining water and proceed with bread baking. Will make 10 to 12 loaves of bread.

YEAST CAKES

Yeast cakes and dried yeast have better keeping qualities than the liquid yeast and sponges, which must be used and renewed every week to 10 days. Properly cured yeast cakes will keep for several weeks. Dried yeast will keep two to three months. Either can be used to make a starter batch of liquid yeast or sponge.

HOPS YEAST CAKES

Cook 1 medium potato and ¼ cup hops in 3 cups water until potato is well done. Drain, reserving liquid and discarding hops. Add cold water to liquid to make 2½ cups. Into this mix ¼ cup flour and ½ cup corn meal, stirring to make a stiff paste. Cool, then roll into cakes, using 2 tablespoons paste for each cake. Dip each cake in corn meal and roll until easily handled. Dry for several days on a wire rack, turning daily. When perfectly dry, store in a cool place.

To keep even longer, stir in more corn meal until yeast becomes a hard dough. Make into small, thin cakes and dry perfectly without baking or cooking. These cakes keep for several months.

STARTER YEAST CAKES

Mix 2 cups starter, 5 cups warm water, 5 tablespoons shortening, 5 tablespoons honey, 1 tablespoon salt and 4 cups flour until thoroughly blended into a thin batter. Pour into a warm 1-gallon crock. Cover and let rise in a warm place overnight. In the morning, reserve 1 cup for future starter and to the rest add enough corn meal to make a stiff dough. Pat into small, round patties and dry on a wire rack.

BUTTERMILK YEAST CAKES

Scald 2 cups buttermilk, but do not boil. Cool to lukewarm. Add 1 cup yeast and enough flour to make a batter. Set to rise for 24 hours. Stir down. Add enough corn meal to make a stiff dough and roll out. Cut into 2-inch squares, ½-inch thick. Use 1 cake for each 4 cups flour.

PEACH LEAF YEAST CAKES

Peel and boil 3 medium potatoes with ½ cup peach leaves in water to cover. Remove potatoes, mash, then pour the water in which they were boiled back over them, straining off and discarding the peach leaves. Cool potatoes to lukewarm and add 1 cup yeast starter, 1 teaspoon sugar, ½ teaspoon salt and let rise in a warm place overnight. In the morning, stir in enough flour to make a very stiff batter. Let rise again 1 to 2 hours. Stir down. Add enough flour to make a dough, roll out to 1/3-inch thick and cut into 2-inch squares. Place on a wire rack to dry in the shade. Turn every day and take inside at night. To use, dissolve yeast in lukewarm water and use 1 cake for every 4 cups flour.

DRIED YEAST

DRIED HOPS YEAST

Boil 4 ounces hops in 4 quarts water for ½ hour. Strain, pouring water into a large mixing bowl. Discard hops. Cool water to lukewarm. Add 8 cups rye flour, mix well and add 3 cups yeast starter. Let stand in a warm room, covered, overnight. In the morning, stir down and add 16 cups barley flour. Roll out very thin and cut into squares. Dry in the open air, away from the sun and break into small pieces. Crumble on absorbent paper and dry thoroughly. Package in not-too-tightly closed containers, and store in a cool place. Do not allow to freeze.

DRIED POTATO YEAST

Boil 2 large potatoes and a handful of hops tied in a bag, in 3 pints water. Take out potatoes when done, mash well and add 2 cups flour. Pour the boiling water (strain off the

hops) over this and beat well. Add 1 tablespoon salt, 1 tablespoon ginger and ½ cup sugar. When lukewarm add 1 cup yeast and let set 2 days (1 day in very warm weather), stirring down frequently.

At the end of this time add enough white corn meal to make thick enough to form into cakes about ½ inch thick. Place to dry in the shade where the air will pass over the cakes freely and dry them as soon as possible. Turn frequently, breaking them up somewhat or crumbling them until dry. When thoroughly dried, hang in a paper sack.

DRIED ALUM YEAST

To 2 cups flour add enough boiling water to make a thick batter. Stir until smooth, then cool to lukewarm. Add 1 teaspoon powdered alum, 1 teaspoon salt, 1 tablespoon sugar and ½ cup yeast starter. Cover and set in a warm place to ferment, 4 to 6 hours. Stir down and work in enough corn meal to make a stiff dough. Spread out on cookie sheet. Dry in a well-ventilated place out of the sun.

To use, dissolve 1 tablespoon of the powder in 1 cup warm water and use in place of 1 cup yeast starter.

SPONGES

SPONGE (OR STARTER) FOR WINTER USE

Peel and boil 4 or 5 medium sized potatoes in 2 quarts water. When tender, mash very fine in the crock in which the sponge is to be made. Make a well in the center and place 1 cup flour in this. Pour over this 1 quart boiling water from the potatoes. Add ¼ cup sugar and stir thoroughly. Cool. Add 2 cups lukewarm water, enough flour to make a thin batter and 1 cup yeast starter. Let rise 4 hours. Stir down and add enough flour to make a smooth dough. Knead 10 minutes. Let rise again. Punch down. Mold into loaves and put in bread pans. Let rise until double in bulk. Bake.

LIGHT BREAD YEAST

Boil and mash 6 potatoes. Add 2 tablespoons honey, 2 tablespoons butter, 1 quart lukewarm water left from the potatoes and 3 cups flour. Beat to a smooth batter. Add ½ cup yeast starter. Let rise overnight. In the morning, knead in sufficient flour to make a stiff, spongy dough. Knead vigorously 15 minutes and set to rise. When light, knead for 10 minutes. Mold into loaves and let rise again. Bake.

SPONGE-STARTER BREAD

Pour 1¼ cups boiling water over 1½ cups flour. Add 4 tablespoons honey, 1 tablespoon salt and 2 cups water cool

enough to make the mixture lukewarm. Add 1 cup yeast starter. Cover and let stand overnight in a warm place. In the morning, stir down and reserve 2 cups to refrigerate for the next batch. To the rest add ½ cup sugar, 1 quart lukewarm water, 7 cups flour and beat well with a spoon. Set in a warm place to rise. After 1 hour, stir down, add 1 tablespoon salt, 2 cups lukewarm water and 8 cups flour. Mix well. Turn out on a floured board and knead 10 minutes, or until smooth and elastic. Let rise again until doubled in bulk. Knead lightly again. Shape into 4 loaves and place in greased bread pans. Let rise again until doubled in bulk. Bake.

EVERLASTING SPONGE

Mix 2 cups flour, 1 cup sugar, ½ cup starter and enough lukewarm water to make a batter. Cover and let rise. To make bread, add 1 quart water and enough flour to make a stiff batter. Beat 100 strokes. Let rise and take out 1 pint of sponge to save for the next batch. Store in a cool place. Add salt to the rest of the sponge and knead dough 10 minutes. Let rise, mold into loaves, let rise again and bake. The oftener the yeast is used, the better the bread.

"SPOOK" YEAST

2 to 3 medium potatoes
1 cup yeast starter
water

4 tablespoons sugar
1 tablespoon salt
flour

Boil potatoes in water to cover. Pour off 1 pint water and cool to lukewarm. Add yeast, 2 tablespoons sugar and pour into a quart glass jar. Let stand 2 days. When ready to bake, pour more water into the "spook" to fill the jar and let stand 8 hours. In the evening take out ½ the yeast and use it to start the bread. Add to it 1 quart warm water, 2 tablespoons sugar and the salt. Mix in enough flour to make a stiff dough and knead well. Let rise overnight. In the morning, it is ready to form into loaves. To the yeast in the jar, do not add salt, but add 2 tablespoons sugar and store in a cool place. At the next baking, proceed as before.

SUGAR SPONGE

7 tablespoons bread sponge
7 tablespoons sugar
1 pint warm water

flour
1 teaspoon salt
4 tablespoons lard

To start yeast, take any kind of bread sponge, place in a quart jar and add 6 tablespoons sugar. Put away until your next baking. The evening before baking bread, put the yeast into the warm water and add enough flour to make a stiff batter. Let stand until morning and put back 7 table- spoons of this sponge in the jar with 6 tablespoons sugar.

Store in a cool place. To the remainder of the sponge, add 1 tablespoon sugar, the salt, lard and enough flour to make a stiff dough. Knead 10 minutes. Let rise until doubled, mold into loaves and let rise again. Bake in a moderate oven. Makes 2 loaves.

YEAST WITHOUT YEAST

Yes, I know I said, "You'll need seed," but some people say they can make yeast without yeast. To prove it, they gave me some recipes. I tried them and failed, and we've talked to other folks who say it can't be done.

But in case you want to try, I've included a couple of the recipes. I won't guarantee anything, but they might work for you.

HOPS YEAST WITHOUT YEAST

On Monday morning, boil 1 pint hops in 2 gallons of water for ½ hour. Strain into a crock and let the liquid become lukewarm. Add 1 teaspoon salt and 1 cup brown sugar. Mix in 1 cup flour with some of the liquid and beat until smooth. Stir thoroughly, cover with a cloth and set in a warm place.

On Wednesday, add 3 pounds potatoes boiled and mashed. Stir well and let stand until Thursday.

Then strain and put in stone jugs. For the first day or two, leave the corks loose. Stir occasionally and keep in a warm place. It should be made two weeks before using and will keep any length of time, improving with age. Keep in a cool

place and shake the jug well just before u ▮
for two loaves of bread.

MILK To 1 quart of fresh, warm milk add ½ te▬
YEAST sugar and enough flour to make a thick
put in a warm place until it beco▬
immediately to make two loaves of brea▬

OTHER OLD-FASHIONED "I▬

SOUR DOUGH Combine 1 cup rye flour, ½ cup luke▬
STARTER cup yeast starter (or ½ package dried y▬
cup lukewarm water.) Keep at room tem▬
until it attains the desired sourness. U▬
bread, reserving 1 cup as a starter for t▬

  OR
Boil 4 medium potatoes which have▬
cubed. Mash in water they were boiled ▬
rye flour, ½ cup honey and 2 teaspoons ▬
well. Pour into a large crock, cover with a▬
ble for 4 days before using.

  OR
Sour 1 cup milk by letting it stand at
for 1 day. Then stir in 1 cup flour, the ▬
covered in a warm place for 3 days.

  OR
Mix 4 cups flour, 1 teaspoon salt, 1 cu▬
poons sugar with enough warm wate▬
batter. Let stand 24 hours.

water to lukewarm. Add 8 cups rye flour, mix well and add 3 cups yeast starter. Let stand in a warm room, covered, overnight. In the morning, stir down and add 16 cups barley flour. Roll out very thin and cut into squares. Dry in the open air, away from the sun and break into small pieces. Crumble on absorbent paper and dry thoroughly. Package in not-too-tightly closed containers, and store in a cool place. Do not allow to freeze.

DRIED POTATO YEAST

Boil 2 large potatoes and a handful of hops tied in a bag, in 3 pints water. Take out potatoes when done, mash well and add 2 cups flour. Pour the boiling water (strain off the

hops) over this and beat well. Add 1 tablespoon salt, 1 tablespoon ginger and ½ cup sugar. When lukewarm add 1 cup yeast and let set 2 days (1 day in very warm weather), stirring down frequently.

At the end of this time add enough white corn meal to make thick enough to form into cakes about ½ inch thick. Place to dry in the shade where the air will pass over the cakes freely and dry them as soon as possible. Turn frequently, breaking them up somewhat or crumbling them until dry. When thoroughly dried, hang in a paper sack.

DRIED ALUM YEAST

To 2 cups flour add enough boiling water to make a thick batter. Stir until smooth, then cool to lukewarm. Add 1 teaspoon powdered alum, 1 teaspoon salt, 1 tablespoon sugar and ½ cup yeast starter. Cover and set in a warm place to ferment, 4 to 6 hours. Stir down and work in enough corn meal to make a stiff dough. Spread out on cookie sheet. Dry in a well-ventilated place out of the sun.

To use, dissolve 1 tablespoon of the powder in 1 cup warm water and use in place of 1 cup yeast starter.

SPONGES

SPONGE (OR STARTER) FOR WINTER USE

Peel and boil 4 or 5 medium sized potatoes in 2 quarts water. When tender, mash very fine in the crock in which the sponge is to be made. Make a well in the center and place 1 cup flour in this. Pour over this 1 quart boiling water from the potatoes. Add ¼ cup sugar and stir thoroughly. Cool. Add 2 cups lukewarm water, enough flour to make a thin batter and 1 cup yeast starter. Let rise 4 hours. Stir down and add enough flour to make a smooth dough. Knead 10 minutes. Let rise again. Punch down. Mold into loaves and put in bread pans. Let rise until double in bulk. Bake.

LIGHT BREAD YEAST

Boil and mash 6 potatoes. Add 2 tablespoons honey, 2 tablespoons butter, 1 quart lukewarm water left from the potatoes and 3 cups flour. Beat to a smooth batter. Add ½ cup yeast starter. Let rise overnight. In the morning, knead in sufficient flour to make a stiff, spongy dough. Knead vigorously 15 minutes and set to rise. When light, knead for 10 minutes. Mold into loaves and let rise again. Bake.

SPONGE-STARTER BREAD

Pour 1¼ cups boiling water over 1½ cups flour. Add 4 tablespoons honey, 1 tablespoon salt and 2 cups water cool

enough to make the mixture lukewarm. Add 1 cup yeast starter. Cover and let stand overnight in a warm place. In the morning, stir down and reserve 2 cups to refrigerate for the next batch. To the rest add ½ cup sugar, 1 quart lukewarm water, 7 cups flour and beat well with a spoon. Set in a warm place to rise. After 1 hour, stir down, add 1 tablespoon salt, 2 cups lukewarm water and 8 cups flour. Mix well. Turn out on a floured board and knead 10 minutes, or until smooth and elastic. Let rise again until doubled in bulk. Knead lightly again. Shape into 4 loaves and place in greased bread pans. Let rise again until doubled in bulk. Bake.

EVERLASTING SPONGE

Mix 2 cups flour, 1 cup sugar, ½ cup starter and enough lukewarm water to make a batter. Cover and let rise. To make bread, add 1 quart water and enough flour to make a stiff batter. Beat 100 strokes. Let rise and take out 1 pint of sponge to save for the next batch. Store in a cool place. Add salt to the rest of the sponge and knead dough 10 minutes. Let rise, mold into loaves, let rise again and bake. The oftener the yeast is used, the better the bread.

"SPOOK"
YEAST

2 to 3 medium potatoes   4 tablespoons sugar
1 cup yeast starter   1 tablespoon salt
water   flour

Boil potatoes in water to cover. Pour off 1 pint water and cool to lukewarm. Add yeast, 2 tablespoons sugar and pour into a quart glass jar. Let stand 2 days. When ready to bake, pour more water into the "spook" to fill the jar and let stand 8 hours. In the evening take out ½ the yeast and use it to start the bread. Add to it 1 quart warm water, 2 tablespoons sugar and the salt. Mix in enough flour to make a stiff dough and knead well. Let rise overnight. In the morning, it is ready to form into loaves. To the yeast in the jar, do not add salt, but add 2 tablespoons sugar and store in a cool place. At the next baking, proceed as before.

SUGAR
SPONGE

7 tablespoons bread sponge   flour
7 tablespoons sugar   1 teaspoon salt
1 pint warm water   4 tablespoons lard

To start yeast, take any kind of bread sponge, place in a quart jar and add 6 tablespoons sugar. Put away until your next baking. The evening before baking bread, put the yeast into the warm water and add enough flour to make a stiff batter. Let stand until morning and put back 7 tablespoons of this sponge in the jar with 6 tablespoons sugar.

Store in a cool place. To the remainder of the sponge, add 1 tablespoon sugar, the salt, lard and enough flour to make a stiff dough. Knead 10 minutes. Let rise until doubled, mold into loaves and let rise again. Bake in a moderate oven. Makes 2 loaves.

YEAST WITHOUT YEAST

Yes, I know I said, "You'll need seed," but some people say they can make yeast without yeast. To prove it, they gave me some recipes. I tried them and failed, and we've talked to other folks who say it can't be done.

But in case you want to try, I've included a couple of the recipes. I won't guarantee anything, but they might work for you.

HOPS YEAST WITHOUT YEAST

On Monday morning, boil 1 pint hops in 2 gallons of water for ½ hour. Strain into a crock and let the liquid become lukewarm. Add 1 teaspoon salt and 1 cup brown sugar. Mix in 1 cup flour with some of the liquid and beat until smooth. Stir thoroughly, cover with a cloth and set in a warm place.

On Wednesday, add 3 pounds potatoes boiled and mashed. Stir well and let stand until Thursday.

Then strain and put in stone jugs. For the first day or two, leave the corks loose. Stir occasionally and keep in a warm place. It should be made two weeks before using and will keep any length of time, improving with age. Keep in a cool place and shake the jug well just before using. Use one cup for two loaves of bread.

MILK YEAST   To 1 quart of fresh, warm milk add ½ teaspoon salt, ¼ cup sugar and enough flour to make a thick batter. Cover and put in a warm place until it becomes light. Use it immediately to make two loaves of bread.

OTHER OLD-FASHIONED "RISINGS"

SOUR DOUGH STARTER   Combine 1 cup rye flour, ½ cup lukewarm water and ½ cup yeast starter (or ½ package dried yeast dissolved in ½ cup lukewarm water.) Keep at room temperature 2 or 3 days until it attains the desired sourness. Use for sour dough bread, reserving 1 cup as a starter for the next batch.

OR

Boil 4 medium potatoes which have been peeled and cubed. Mash in water they were boiled in and add 4 cups rye flour, ½ cup honey and 2 teaspoons salt, the yeast. Mix well. Pour into a large crock, cover with a towel and let bubble for 4 days before using.

OR

Sour 1 cup milk by letting it stand at room temperature for 1 day. Then stir in 1 cup flour, the yeast and leave uncovered in a warm place for 3 days.

OR

Mix 4 cups flour, 1 teaspoon salt, 1 cup yeast and 2 tablespoons sugar with enough warm water to make a thick batter. Let stand 24 hours.

24

BAKING POWDERS

Grandmother used a spoonful of bicarbonate of soda with ½ ounce of vinegar to make her cakes high and light. Lemon juice and soda will also make cakes and quick breads rise. But both require a strong arm and a quick hand. They are not for the beginner. However, all baking powder doughs must be mixed quickly in order to get a light, fine-grained dough.

Cream of tartar and soda, when mixed with dough, act more slowly than tartaric acid and soda. When cream of tartar and soda are to be used for baking powder, allow 1 teaspoon soda to three teaspoons cream of tartar for each cup of flour. One-half teaspoon soda to 1 cup buttermilk or sour milk will raise 2 cups flour.

TARTARIC ACID POWDER

Mix ¾ pound of tartaric acid, 1 pound bicarbonate of soda, 6 ounces flour or cornstarch. Sift 5 or 6 times. Store in a dry place. Use 2 tablespoons for each cup of flour.

OR

Thoroughly mix 16 ounces cornstarch, 8 ounces bicarbonate of soda and 5 ounces tartaric acid. Use with sour milk or buttermilk to a proportion of 3 teaspoons per cup of flour.

CREAM OF TARTAR POWDER   Combine 1 pound bicarbonate of soda, 2 pounds cream of tartar and 10 ounces cornstarch or flour. Sift 5 or 6 times and store in a tightly-covered jar. Use 2 teaspoons per cup of flour.

BREAD RECIPES

The following bread recipes can be used with any of the home-grown yeast recipes beginning on Page 11. If you prefer, you may substitute 1 yeast cake (or 1 package of dry yeast) dissolved in warm water, for each cup of yeast called for in the recipe.

Since home-ground wheat flours vary greatly in their absorption of liquids, the amount of wheat in each of the recipes is only approximate. You may have to add more or less flour as indicated.

WHEAT BREADS

Even if you've made bread before, the first time you use whole grains, you may be in for a few surprises. In general:

Expect a few failures. Freshly-ground, whole grains are harder to work with than the commercial varieties. Ease of handling is one reason most of the nutrition is deleted from wheat before putting it on the grocer's shelf. The whole grain dough tends to be sticky no matter how much flour you add. It is also slower to rise, but more likely to fall. No matter. A few bad batches is the price of learning. Besides, if you have a few chickens, a bad batch can be a bonus. Chickens relish whole grain bread, and it's far better — and cheaper — feed than the commercial protein supplements.

Expect foods made of fresh whole grains to mold and ferment if not refrigerated or eaten within a few days. There are no preservatives in them to lengthen the shelf life.

Don't expect homemade whole wheat bread to be light and fluffy like the store-bought variety. It isn't supposed to be. Your loaves will be smaller and heavier, browner and crunchier.

Do expect it to be delicious and nutritious and well worth the trouble.

Note: In the recipes which follow the yeast ingredient given refers to liquid yeast starter. Refer to the section on Home Grown Yeasts beginning on Page 11.

WHOLE WHEAT BREAD

2 cups milk	3 tablespoons honey
3 tablespoons lard or butter	2 eggs
1 teaspoon salt	2 cups yeast

12 cups (about) freshly-ground wheat flour

Scald milk. Pour into a large mixing bowl (a heavy crockery bowl keeps an even temperature for better rising). Add shortening and salt. Cool to lukewarm and add honey and yeast. Mix well. Add eggs and beat well with an egg beater. Add 3 cups flour and beat 100 strokes. Add 3 cups more flour and repeat. Now add enough flour to make a dough that can be handled. Remove to a surface which has been covered with flour.

Knead 10 minutes, or until you can feel the dough tighten and become elastic. The dough will be slightly sticky. Don't skimp on the kneading; it's the most important step. When the dough springs back, grease it with your hands, place it in a warmed, well-greased crockery bowl and cover it with a slightly-damp cloth. Let set in a warm, draft-free place for 1 to 1½ hours, or until doubled in bulk.

When the dough is double in size, punch down and divide into four equal portions. Liberally grease four bread pans and shape the dough into four small loaves. Let rise again in a warm place about 1 hour, or until the loaves have risen just above the top of the pans. They should be the size of the finished loaves at this point. Bake in a pre-heated 350-degree (moderate) oven for 1 hour, or until golden brown. Let cool at least one half hour before slicing.

MIXED GRAIN BREAD

Scald 2 cups milk. Pour 1 cup of it over 3 tablespoons lard in a large mixing bowl. Stir to dissolve lard. Allow remaining cup milk to cool, then combine with ½ cup soy beans in electric blender and blend at high speed. Add this mixture to other milk mixture and add 1 teaspoon salt, 3 tablespoons honey, 2 beaten eggs and 2 cups liquid yeast.

In another mixing bowl, combine 8 cups wheat, 2 cups rolled oats, 1 cup rye berries and 1 cup shelled corn. Grind to a fine flour in grain mill. Add 6 cups of this flour to milk mixture and beat 100 strokes. Add remaining flour to make a dough that is easily handled. You will need more wheat flour for kneading. Knead 10 minutes, then set in a well-greased bowl in a warm, draft-free place. Cover and let rise until doubled in bulk — about 1½ hours.

When doubled, punch down and divide into four equal portions. Shape into loaves and place in greased loaf pans. Let rise 1 hour and bake in a 350-degree oven.

BROWN BREAD

1 cup corn meal	1½ teaspoons salt
1 cup wheat flour	½ cup molasses
1 cup rye flour	2 cups sour milk
	1½ teaspoons soda

Mix dry ingredients together. Sift and mix again. Add molasses and sour milk and beat well. Pour into buttered molds (or tin cans) and steam 3 hours. If you want a crust, remove bread from molds and bake 15 minutes on a cookie sheet.

OR:

Combine 1 quart bread sponge (Page 20) and ½ cup molasses. Stir in enough freshly-ground wheat flour to make a stiff dough. Knead until elastic. Grease a deep pan and set the dough to rise. When light, put bread pan over a kettle of hot water (keep bread well covered) and steam for ½ hour. Then bake in moderate (350-degree) oven until done.

WHEAT-RYE BREAD

8 cups rye flour
4 cups wheat flour
2 cups yeast
4 cups warm water
2 teaspoons salt
4 tablespoons lard
3 tablespoons honey

Mix the flours with the salt. Stir in warm water, yeast and honey. Beat batter thoroughly, Dough will be sticky, but must be kept soft. Pour into 4 well-greased pans and set in a

warm place to rise 1 to 2 hours, until doubled in bulk. Bake 45 to 55 minutes in a moderate (350-degree) oven. While still hot, rub the crust with butter to soften.

NINETYTHREE
NINETYFOUR
NINETYFI...

WHEAT-OATMEAL BREAD

½ cup rolled oats   ½ teaspoon salt
1½ cups wheat flour   1 cup yeast
2 cups boiling water   ½ tablespoon butter
½ cup molasses

In a mixing bowl, pour the boiling water over the oats and let stand until lukewarm. Add salt, butter, yeast and molasses. Stir in flour and beat thoroughly. Set to rise in greased bread pan. When doubled in bulk, bake in moderate oven (350-degree) for 1 hour.

WINTER MORNING BREAD

4 cups milk   1 tablespoon lard or butter
1 teaspoon salt   3 eggs
1 cup yeast   1 cup rolled oats, ground
½ cup honey   home ground wheat

Scald milk and pour over shortening and salt in large mixing bowl. Let cool. Stir in honey, yeast, eggs and oats which have been ground with 2 cups wheat. Beat well and let set

10 minutes. Add enough wheat flour to make soft dough. Beat well again. Pour into a shallow cake pan and cover loosely. Let set in a draft-free place overnight. In the morning, if the kitchen was not too warm, it should be ready to bake in a moderate oven (350-degree) for 1 hour. Serve hot.

SALT RISING BREAD

4 tablespoons corn meal	1 cup fresh milk
2 tablespoons honey	1 cup potato water
1½ tablespoons salt	2 tablespoons lard

5¼ cups home ground whole wheat flour

The day before baking, scald milk, cool and add one-half of the honey and the salt. Stir in corn meal. Place bowl in a pan of warm water, cover and let stand in a warm place overnight. Next morning, stir in warm potato water, the rest of the honey, the lard and 2 cups flour. Beat well. Place bowl in a pan of warm water, cover and let rise. When doubled in bulk, turn into a warm mixing bowl and slowly add remainder of flour. Knead 10 minutes. Place in greased bread pans, cover and let rise. Bake 35 to 45 minutes in moderate oven (350-degrees).

FRENCH BREAD

(This is not, strictly speaking, a true French bread, since the French traditionally make their bread of a creamy white flour. If you want a true French bread, you may use white flour only and come close. But we like it this way.

2 cups lukewarm yeast	2 tablespoons soft lard
4 cups unbleached flour	2 tablespoons honey
1 teaspoon salt	3 cups home-ground wheat flour

Combine yeast, salt, honey and lard, mixing well. Add yeast and one-half of each of the flours. Beat 100 strokes. Stir in remaining flours and knead 10 minutes, until smooth and elastic. Dough will be soft. Place in a greased bowl, cover and let rise about 1 hour, until doubled in bulk. Punch down dough and let rise again about ½ hour. Punch down again and divide into two portions. Roll each portion into an oblong about 8 by 10 inches. Roll up tightly into a long loaf and seal by pinching edges together. Place on a greased baking sheet which has been sprinkled lightly with corn meal. Brush loaves with a glaze made of 1 teaspoon cornstarch combined with ½ cup cold water, then cooked to a smooth thickness. Let loaves rise, uncovered, about 1½ hours. Again brush with glaze and, with sharp knife, cut slashes at 2-inch intervals. Bake 10 minutes in hot (400-degree) oven. Remove from oven, brush with glaze, bake at 350 degrees another 30 minutes to golden brown.

BREAD STICKS

1 cup milk	¼ cup lard or butter
1 tablespoon honey	1 cup yeast
½ teaspoon salt	1 egg
	4 to 5 cups wheat flour

Scald milk and pour over lard and salt in a mixing bowl. Stir well, then let cool to lukewarm. Add honey, beaten egg, yeast and enough flour to make a dough. Knead 10 minutes, then place in a warmed, greased bowl and cover. Let rise 1½ hours, or until doubled in bulk. Punch down and, working with small pieces at a time, roll into bread sticks. Place on a greased cookie sheet and let rise again. Bake in 300-degree oven until golden.

RUSKS

1 cup yeast	4 eggs
1 cup raw sugar	½ cup lard
1 cup cream	½ cup butter

Freshly-ground whole wheat flour

Combine first four ingredients with enough flour to make a thin batter. Beat 100 strokes. Add more flour to make a thick batter and let rise 1 hour. Add ½ cup softened butter and ½ cup softened lard, combined. Add more flour to make a dough that can be handled. Roll out to ½-inch thick and cut as for large biscuits. Place on cookie sheet and let rise in a warm place 1 hour. Bake in 350-degree oven until light brown. Cool, then slice and dry in a 200-degree oven until golden brown and toasted throughout.

CORN BREADS

RYE AND INDIAN BREAD

(This is a very old recipe, written when ground corn was still known as Indian Meal.)

2 cups yellow corn meal, finely ground
2 cups boiling water
½ cup yeast

½ cup honey
1 teaspoon salt
½ teaspoon soda
2 cups ground rye

cold water

Put the corn meal in a mixing bowl and add boiling water. Let set 10 minutes, then add enough cold water to make soft batter. Cool to lukewarm, add yeast, honey, salt, soda, rye flour. Beat thoroughly, cover and set in a warm place to rise overnight. When the surface cracks open, stir down and turn into a greased, floured loaf pan. Sprinkle top with flour to keep crust from forming. Let rise again until cracks appear, then bake in moderate oven (350-degrees) 2 to 3 hours, covering with a lid after the first ½ hour.

NORTHERN CORNBREAD

1 cup corn meal
1 cup home-ground wheat flour
½ cup honey
½ teaspoon salt

3 tablespoons baking powder
1 egg
¼ cup lard or butter
1 cup milk

Combine dry ingredients in a mixing bowl. In another bowl, combine beaten egg, honey, milk. Pour over dry ingredients and mix thoroughly. Add melted lard or butter. Stir just enough to blend. Bake in greased 8-inch square pan 25 minutes in moderately hot (400-degree) oven.

EGG SPOON BREAD

3 eggs   2 cups milk
1 cup corn meal   3 tablespoons lard
1½ teaspoons salt 1 cup cold water

    Mix corn meal and salt in mixing bowl. Add cold water and stir until smooth. Add hot milk and lard, stir and cook over low heat until mixture thickens. Blend a small amount of the beaten eggs. Combine all ingredients and pour into a well-greased baking dish and bake 45 to 50 minutes in moderately hot (400-degree) oven.

SPIDER CORNBREAD

1 cup corn meal   1 teaspoon salt
½ cup rolled oats   2 eggs
1 teaspoon soda   2 cups sour milk
                  2 tablespoons lard

    Mix the dry ingredients, add eggs and milk. Melt shortening in an iron spider (skillet) and add to batter. Mix well. Heat spider on top burner, then pour in batter. Cook on medium heat on stove top for 3 minutes. Place in 400-degree oven and bake 15 to 20 minutes. Serve hot with butter.

OTHER BREADS

    Gems — Grandmother's gems were baked in shallow, round gem pans. The best ones were made of heavy iron. If you cannot find the fluted gem pans you may substitute well-greased muffin pans by filling them only 1/3 full.

CORN GEMS

1 cup corn meal	½ cup honey
1 cup wheat flour	2 eggs
1 cup milk	2 teaspoons baking powder
½ cup lard	½ teaspoon salt

Beat eggs well, then add honey and melted lard. Combine with milk and add corn meal, salt and baking powder and flour. Bake in greased, hot gem pans 15 minutes in 400-degree oven.

OATMEAL GEMS

Soak 2 cups oatmeal overnight in 2 cups milk. In the morning, add the yolks of 2 well-beaten eggs, 2 tablespoons honey, ½ teaspoon salt and the egg whites beaten stiffly. Mix gently and bake 20 minutes at 350 degrees in greased, hot gem pans.

WHOLE WHEAT GEMS

Mix 2 teaspoons baking powder with 2 cups whole wheat flour. Add the yolks of 2 eggs, 1 tablespoon butter, 1 cup milk and ½ teaspoon salt. Mix well, then blend in 2 stiffly-beaten egg whites. Bake in greased, hot gem pans about 20 minutes.

CRACKERS AND CAKES

YEAST CRACKERS

2 cups lukewarm water	½ cup yeast
½ teaspoon salt	5 to 6 cups ground wheat flour

Add water to salt and yeast. Stir to mix thoroughly. Add enough flour to make dough. Turn out on board and knead, adding flour as you go, to make a stiff dough. When smooth, place in a greased bowl to rise until double in bulk.

Then put back on kneading board and roll out very thin, using small pieces of dough to work with. Cut into squares with crisscross slices and place separated squares on greased cookie sheet. Perforate with fork tines, then sprinkle lightly with salt. Bake immediately, without rising, in moderate oven (350-degrees) until edges begin to brown. Will keep several days in a warm, dry place. May need rewarming to crisp before serving.

OR:

Use scraps from any bread dough. Roll paper thin, cut

into squares, perforate through with fork and bake in hot oven (400-degree) until beginning to brown.

PLAIN CRACKERS   To 4 cups flour made of mixed grains, add 1 tablespoon lard and 1 teaspoon salt. Mix to the consistency of meal. Add water to make a stiff paste. Beat 100 strokes, or until paste blisters. Add flour to make a stiff dough, roll thin and cut into squares. Perforate with fork and bake in hot oven (400 degrees) until crisp.

SODA CRACKERS

4 cups flour	1 egg
1 tablespoon lard	1 teaspoon salt
	1 teaspoon soda

Mix dry ingredients and cut in lard to the consistency of corn meal. Add beaten egg and enough buttermilk to make a stiff paste and beat well. Roll thin on floured board, cut in squares and perforate with fork. Bake in hot oven (400 degrees) until crisp.

HUNTSVILLE CRACKERS

To 2 cups risen bread dough, add 1 tablespoon honey, 1 egg, 1 tablespoon butter, 1 tablespoon lard and 1 tablespoon soda dissolved in 1 cup of cream. Beat 5 minutes, adding more flour to make a stiff dough. Roll out thin, cut in squares and bake in hot oven.

GRAHAM CRACKERS

To 4 cups graham flour (or 4 cups freshly ground whole wheat flour) add 3 tablespoons honey, 2 teaspoons baking powder, 1 teaspoon salt and enough water to make a stiff dough. Knead 10 minutes. Roll thin, cut in squares and bake in moderate oven. When lightly brown, remove and cool, then put back in warm (200-degree) oven and dry until crisp but not too brown. Can be crumpled and served with milk as a cereal or eaten as graham crackers.

RYE CAKES WITH HONEY

2 cups sour milk	2 teaspoons soda
2 cups rye flour	2 eggs
½ teaspoon salt	½ cup honey

Dissolve the soda in the sour milk, add flour and salt, beat to make a thin batter. Add well-beaten eggs. Add honey and beat well. Bake on a hot, well-greased griddle. Serve with butter and honey.

CORN CAKES

2 cups buttermilk	½ teaspoon soda
1 egg	½ teaspoon salt
2 tablespoons butter	corn meal

Combine ingredients, then add enough corn meal to make a soft batter. Bake on a hot, well-greased griddle. Serve with butter and honey.

FLANNEL CAKES

1½ cups corn meal	2 tablespoons honey
1½ cups wheat flour	4 tablespoons lard
1 teaspoon salt	1 cup yeast
3 cups milk	

Scald milk and pour over corn meal in mixing bowl. Add honey, salt, and lard and stir well. Cool to lukewarm, then add remaining ingredients. Let rise overnight. In the morning, cook as griddle cakes.

OTHER WHOLE GRAINS RECIPES

CRACKED WHEAT BREAKFAST CEREAL

To 2 quarts boiling water, add 2 cups cracked wheat (a quick trip through the blender cracks it just right). Stir in wheat slowly, turn down heat and stir until it begins to thicken. Add ½ teaspoon salt if you like. Cover and lower heat. Cook slowly 1 hour, stirring occasionally. Serve hot with cream and honey. Pour any leftovers into a bread pan. When cold and set, slice and fry as mush.

WHEAT SCRAPPLE

Cook coarsely-ground wheat or corn or a combination of the two in a proportion of 2 cups grain to 2 quarts boiling water. Cook slowly 1 hour, then mix with bits of cooked ham, sausage or fresh pork. Season with 1 teaspoon salt, 1 teaspoon sage, ⅛ teaspoon pepper and thyme to taste. Pour into a mold rinsed in cold water and refrigerate overnight. Slice and fry for breakfast.

WHOLE WHEAT NOODLES

Beat 2 eggs with a fork until blended. Add 1 teaspoon salt and 1½ cups whole wheat flour. Mix well. Add enough flour to make a very stiff dough, then turn out on a well-floured board and knead, adding as much flour as possible. Divide into two pieces and roll one piece as thin as possible, sprinkling on flour to keep rolling pin from sticking. Roll out other piece and let both stand 1 hour to dry slightly. Then roll up tightly in two rolls and slice in very thin slices to make noodles. Spread out on floured surface to dry, stirring up occasionally with the hands. Let dry 2 days on a clean towel in a warm kitchen or several hours in the sun outdoors. Will keep indefinitely if thoroughly dried.

POTATO DOUGHNUTS

2 cups milk	1½ cups mashed potatoes
4 tablespoons lard	4 eggs, beaten
½ cup honey	10 to 12 cups wheat flour
1 teaspoon salt	2 cups yeast

Scald milk and pour over lard and salt in large mixing bowl. Stir in mashed potatoes (may be leftovers) and cool to lukewarm. Add honey, eggs, yeast and 3 cups flour. Beat 100 strokes. Add all of the flour and beat thoroughly. You should have a soft, slightly moist dough. Sprinkle 2 cups flour on kneading surface and turn out dough. Knead until dough is soft and pliable. Add 1 or 2 cups more flour if necessary, but dough should still be slightly sticky when kneading is finished. Place in a warmed, greased heavy bowl and cover. Let rise in a warm, draft-free place until doubled in bulk, 1 to 2 hours.

At the end of that time, return to kneading surface and roll to ½ inch thick. Cut for doughnuts and place on greased cookie sheet. Cover and let rise 30 minutes, or until doubled. Fry in hot fat until brown. Drain and add glaze or sugar. Makes about 6 dozen.

PUFFED WHEAT Heat 1 tablespoon oil in a heavy iron skillet. When it is very hot, add ½ cup wheat. Turn off heat. The wheat will pop like corn and may be eaten with milk and honey for breakfast as a cereal or buttered and eaten hot like popcorn.

CONTENTS & INDEX

Growing your own grains   3
  Planting   5
  Harvesting   6
  Storing   7
Raising other grains   7
  Corn   7
  Other sources   8
  Storing   9
  Grinding   9
Home-Grown Yeasts   11
  Sponge or starter   11
  Everlasting yeasts   12
    Potato yeast   12
    Hops yeast   13
    Malt yeast   15
    Farmer's yeast   15
    Bran yeast   16
    Grain yeast   16
    Buttermilk yeast   16
  Yeast cakes   17
    Hops yeast cakes   17
    Starter yeast cakes   17
    Buttermilk yeast cakes   18
    Peach leaf yeast cakes   18
  Dried yeast   18
    Dried hops yeast   18
    Dried potato yeast   19
    Dried alum yeast   20
  Sponges   20
    Sponge for winter use   20

    Light bread yeast   20
    Sponge-starter bread   21
    Everlasting sponge   21
    "Spook" yeast   22
    Sugar sponge   22
  Yeast without yeast   23
    Hops yeast without yeast   23
    Milk yeast   24
  Other old-fashioned risings   24
    Sour dough starter   24
    Baking powders   25
    Tartaric acid powder   25
    Cream of tartar powder   26
Bread Recipes   26
  Wheat Breads   26
    Whole wheat bread   27
    Mixed grain breads   28
    Brown bread   29
    Wheat-rye bread   30
    Wheat-oatmeal bread   31
    Winter morning bread   31
    Salt rising bread   32
    French bread   32
    Bread sticks   33
    Rusks   34
  Corn Breads   35
    Rye & Indian bread   35
    Northern cornbread   35
    Egg spoon bread   36
    Spider cornbread   36

Other Breads   36
   Corn gems   37
   Oatmeal gems   37
   Whole wheat gems   37
Crackers and Cakes   37
   Yeast crackers   37
   Plain crackers   38
   Soda crackers   39
   Huntsville crackers   39
   Graham crackers   39

Rye cakes with honey   39
   Corn cakes   40
   Flannel cakes   40
Other Whole grain recipes   40
   Cracked wheat breakfast cereal   40
   Wheat scrapple   41
   Whole wheat noodles   41
   Potato doughnuts   41
   Puffed wheat   42

44

NOTES

NOTES